WHO IS A PERFECTIONIST?

"Twelve Perspectives on Understanding Perfectionism, From Depression to Happiness, Pros and Cons, Persistence, Overthinking, Overcoming, Genetic Influences, Liberation, and Relationship Dynamics."

Nate Tucker

perfect

/ˈpəːfɪkt / ▸ adjective; having all the required or desirable elements, qualities, or characteristics.

perfection

/pəˈfɛkʃn / ▸ noun [mass noun]; the state or quality of being perfect.

perfectionism

/pəˈfɛkʃənɪz(ə)m / ▸ noun [mass noun]; refusal to accept any standard short of perfection.

perfectionist

/pəˈfɛkʃənɪst / ▸ noun; a person who refuses to accept any standard short of perfection.

imperfection

/ˌɪmpəˈfɛkʃn / ▸ noun; a fault, blemish, or undesirable feature.

Contents

What does a person's perfectionism entail?

Understanding the Psychology Behind Perfectionism

The inclination to hold oneself and others to unreasonably high standards is known as perfectionism. The high standards that perfectionists work so hard to fulfill enable some of them to succeed to great degrees. When they commit errors, some people have poor self-esteem and difficulties going about their regular lives.

Perfectionism is not a mental illness; rather, it is a personality attribute. On the other hand, perfectionistic individuals have a higher risk of developing mental health conditions including anxiety, depression, and eating disorders.

What Perfectionism Means

The inclination to set exceedingly high, rigorous, or "flawless" objectives and to make excessive expectations of oneself and others is the hallmark of the perfectionist personality characteristic.

Those who have perfectionistic tendencies usually have high expectations. These guidelines might apply to almost every aspect of life, including:

- → Artistic or athletic performance
- → Academic successes
- → Professional and/or monetary achievement
- → Timeliness, neatness, organization, and/or orderliness
- → Physical characteristics
- → Health and Fitness
- → Families and relationships
- → Observance of a moral or spiritual code

Aiming for great success isn't inherently a negative thing. Adaptive perfectionism, which includes organization, conscientiousness, aiming high, and setting ambitious objectives, is associated with a successful job as well as good self-esteem, happiness, and a higher level of life satisfaction.

On the other hand, unhealthy maladaptive perfectionism is characterized by an overwhelming need for acceptance from others, irrational expectations, negative self-talk, external pressure, and guilt. Maladaptive perfectionism has been linked to poor relationship outcomes, low self-esteem, and a fear of failing.

Medical Knowledge

Several possible reasons for perfectionism have been identified by medical professionals. The following elements might make you more likely to exhibit perfectionistic qualities:

Genetics: Studies indicate that perfectionism may sometimes run in families. According to twin studies, perfectionistic traits are influenced by environmental and genetic variables.

Upbringing: Perfectionism is associated with high parental expectations, pressure from parents, and strict parenting methods in some kids and teenagers.

Trauma: A lot of individuals who strive for perfection say they were victims of abuse or neglect as kids.

It is not a mental illness to be a perfectionist. On the other hand, pathological perfectionistic inclinations raise your risk of mental health issues such as the following:

Anxiety and depression: Symptoms of perfectionism, anxiety, and depression often coexist. The diagnostic criteria for disorders such as major depressive disorder (MDD) and generalized anxiety disorder (GAD) are much more likely to be met by perfectionists.

Obsessive-compulsive disorder (OCD) is a mental illness characterized by compulsions, which are repeated behaviors someone engages in to cope with their discomfort related to an obsession, and obsessions, which are persistent, unwelcome thoughts. Perfectionism is a feature that is crucial to the development of OCD. Perfectionistic qualities in children and teenagers increase the likelihood that they may have OCD symptoms in the future.

Eating disorders: Anorexia nervosa (AN) and bulimia nervosa (BN) are two eating disorders that have a well-established relationship with perfectionism. According to research, those who are perfectionists are more prone to aim for extreme thinness, experience body or weight dissatisfaction, and attempt to meet unrealistic beauty standards.

Social and Cultural Factors

Perfectionism is often influenced by personal variables, including heredity, prior trauma, and co-occurring mental health issues (such as depression and anxiety).

Perfectionists are more likely to thrive in or be drawn to certain professions, social settings, civilizations, and subcultures. Typical instances consist of:

Colleges and universities: The danger of maladaptive perfectionism is often increased in academic settings. Research has shown that individuals pursuing degrees in fields with high academic demands, including law, medicine, and pharmacy, are more vulnerable to perfectionism.

Sports: There is a lot of pressure on athletes to perform well, which may sometimes be detrimental. According to research, athletes who strive for perfection as well as those who have coaches who do the same are more prone to burnout.

Arts: Artists often face rigorous scrutiny and competition in their line of work. According to 2020 research, professional dancers who were very critical of themselves were more likely to lose interest in and drive for their work.

Social media: Unrealistic societal beauty standards and depictions of the "ideal" body on social media may cause pathological perfectionism and issues with body image, particularly in young women.

Immigration: Individuals may adopt the high standards of performance from their families, especially if they feel pressured to live up to their parents' sacrifices.

Is There An Increase in Perfectionism?

There is evidence to suggest that perfectionism has increased in frequency during the last several decades. In 2019, a meta-analysis of self-demanding behaviors and attitudes across US, UK, and Canadian college students found that perfectionism rates rose dramatically between 1989 and 2016.17

Three Different Forms of Perfectionism

Perfectionism may be broadly classified into three categories by researchers: socially dictated, self-oriented, and other-oriented.

Self-focused

Self-oriented perfectionism is the propensity to hold oneself to unreasonably high standards.

Self-centered perfectionists depend on their accomplishments outside of themselves to make them feel worthwhile and content. They are harsh critics of who they are. Self-directed perfectionists are often very driven, meticulous, and neurotic (prone to worry, anxiety, and obsessive thinking).

Focused on Others

Perfectionists who are other-oriented place a lot of pressure on others—usually a spouse or children—to make up for perceived shortcomings.

For instance, a parent who strives for perfection can be critical of their child's academic progress all the time. Some other-oriented perfectionists try to force someone else to "be the best" at something by acting in a dictatorial manner.

Socially Mandated

Perfectionism which is socially mandated is the belief that you should live up to others' expectations of you.

An individual prone to socially mandated perfectionism, for instance, could have absorbed cultural, societal, or family demands to a greater extent than their peers. Others could be swayed to acquire perfectionistic qualities in a high-stress setting, such as a cutthroat professional area.

Ten Indications That Someone Is Abusing Power

Characteristics and Signs

One of the main symptoms of pathological perfectionism is an overpowering dread of failing.

Establishing unreachable objectives: Those who have a perfectionistic mindset often hold themselves to very high-performance standards. They may even aim for perfection. This starts a vicious cycle where a perfectionist's self-esteem may collapse when they unavoidably fall short of their very high personal standards.

Criticism: Excessive critical judgments of oneself and others are associated with perfectionism. Perfectionists often criticize themselves for little errors and/or have high expectations of other people.

Reassurance-seeking and obsessive thinking: A lot of perfectionists are always reflecting on their previous mistakes or future objectives. They may constantly seek reassurance from partners, mentors, or bosses about their abilities and values to deal with their worries. Conversely, some perfectionists avoid negative criticism by all means because they are so terrified of it.

Overidentification with achievements: Individuals who exhibit perfectionistic qualities often place an excessive amount of weight on evaluations from others and external success indicators, like grades, to support their sense of self-worth and identity. A perfectionist, for instance, would experience extreme remorse, humiliation, guilt, and shame after making a mistake. They might even believe that they are unworthy or call themselves "failures" in life.

Impact on Day-to-Day Living

According to research, a lot of individuals who have perfectionistic inclinations also have greater stress levels, worse psychological well-being, and lower levels of life satisfaction.

Perfectionism may impede key facets of your daily functioning if it is not managed, such as:

Time management: Despite the seeming contradiction, research has shown a connection between perfectionism and several self-defeating behaviors, including procrastination and ineffective time management. Obsessive thinking and fear of failing might cause things to take longer than they should or prevent you from beginning an activity you detest. In addition to hindering creativity, perfectionism may raise self-doubt and fear of taking on new projects.

Relationships: Your capacity to preserve wholesome, excellent relationships may be adversely affected by perfectionism. Your persistent need for validation and assurance, your workaholic habits, or your critical remarks may irritate your spouse, kids, and other loved ones.

Stress levels: Over time, perfectionists are prone to burnout, overextend themselves, and get agitated. Research indicates that medical students who exhibit high degrees of perfectionism are systematically under far higher stress.

Physical and mental health problems: Prolonged stress and a lack of self-care may raise your chance of developing mental and physical health problems, including anxiety and depression, as well as physical ailments like chronic fatigue syndrome (CFS).

Sleep and Perfectionism

According to research, several characteristics of perfectionism—like underlying guilt and shame—may make it difficult for you to obtain a decent night's sleep. Research indicated that there was a substantial positive correlation between perfectionistic tendencies and sleeplessness.

Perfectionism has been connected to several disruptive thought and behavior patterns, including:

Overactivity: People who suffer from perfectionism often exhibit excessive performance-related behaviors and overactivity, such as working excessively, overgrooming, or staying up late studying. This conduct is often ineffective as it might result in fatigue and burnout.

Rumination: Rumination is a kind of compulsive thought that often revolves around a main idea or subject. These unpleasant, time-consuming, and bothersome thoughts might be associated with emotions of guilt over previous errors or anxieties of not accomplishing a certain goal in the case of a perfectionist.

Overly focused on the details: Because they are preoccupied with the little things, perfectionists often get "lost in the weeds" and lose sight of the larger picture. Because of this, even routine activities might seem overwhelming since they don't consider their job done unless it's perfect.

Intolerance: To reach their objectives, perfectionists often create strict regimens or "rules." For instance, they could be scared to miss a single exercise session or sometimes take a break. This rigidity may result in dominating behaviors toward other individuals.

Getting Rid of Perfectionism

Sometimes, striving for perfection may make you do wonderful things. It may, however, also have a detrimental impact on your relationships, general self-perception, and well-being.

If your everyday life is being impeded by perfectionism, here are some strategies to help you get over it:

Make sensible objectives: When your objectives seem unreachable, it may be simple to lose motivation. Make it a point to establish reasonable deadlines for your realistic objectives. Divide each more ambitious objective into manageable steps to prevent feeling overburdened throughout the process.

Experiment and try new things: It might be detrimental to your performance to identify too strongly with how you performed in a particular activity. Taking up a new hobby or interest might help you let go of the concept that you have to be "perfect" all the time, increase your creativity, and learn to accept that errors are inevitable.

Engage in mindfulness: Anxious thoughts, such as dwelling on past transgressions or fretting about the future, are often linked to perfectionism. You may be able to let go of some of those fixations by practicing mindfulness techniques like meditation to keep yourself rooted in the here and now.

Embrace a growing mentality: Having a growth mentality, which sees obstacles and changes as chances for development rather than as dangers to our stability, is a prerequisite for being adaptable.

Try out CBT

A cognitive behavioral therapist may assist you in recognizing your self-defeating thought patterns, making plans for the future you see, encouraging self-acceptance, and growing in self-compassion and empathy for others.

Healthy Routines to Increase Self-Worth

Perfectionism is often closely associated with poor self-worth. Developing self-worth is a crucial first step in conquering the inclination to aim for an impractical goal.

The following are some easy steps you may take to raise your self-esteem:

Maintain contact: Reminding yourself of your good attributes might come from spending quality time with family and friends. Make sure you schedule time to spend with the people you care about in meaningful ways.

Assist others: Increasing your confidence and elevating your mood may be achieved via serving others. Ask a neighbor if they need assistance, volunteer with a neighborhood organization, or offer to perform a favor for a friend or family member.

Face your pessimistic ideas: Take on your self-critical ideas head-on by engaging in journaling. Whenever you catch yourself thinking anything terrible about yourself, write it down. Make a list of three to five positive attributes you like about yourself for each negative idea. This may assist you in creating a more positive, well-rounded self-image.

Make use of uplifting affirmations: It may seem absurd at first, but you may start your day off correctly by saying encouraging things aloud into a mirror before you go to work or by leaving Post-it notes scattered about the home as you do your daily chores.

Ways to Increase Your Confidence

Perfectionism is characterized as the propensity to hold oneself and/or other people to unreasonable standards. Fear of failing, self-criticism, compulsive thinking, needing affirmation, and establishing unrealistic goals are typical characteristics. Perfectionism may be classified into three basic categories: socially dictated, self-oriented, and other-oriented.

Perfectionism is not a mental illness; rather, it is a personality attribute. On the other hand, it is associated with an increased risk of eating disorders, anxiety, depression, and obsessive-compulsive disorder (OCD). It may also result in diminished self-worth and more stress.

Developing self-acceptance, increasing self-compassion, and boosting self-esteem are usually necessary to overcome perfectionism. Cognitive behavioral therapy (CBT) is one kind of talk therapy that may help break negative thought patterns and increase self-confidence.

The concept of perfectionism is defined in the chapter as the quality of tendency to set unattainably high standards for oneself and others. Although not a mental illness in itself, perfectionism can be a cause for many other mental issues, including anxiety, depression, and eating disorders. It is also categorized in the chapter as adaptive – leading to success – and maladaptive, in the form of irrational expectations and self-talk. Perfectionism has many factors contributing to its development, from genetics and upbringing to trauma. It can affect various aspects of life such as academic performance, relationships, and physical health.

The chapter also describes the rise in perfectionism in recent years, as well as three types of it: self-focused, other-focused, and socially prescribed. Fear of failing, unachievable goal-setting, frequent self-criticism, and reassurance-seeking behavior are traits of perfectionism. It affects relationships, day-to-day activities, stress, and sleep. Cognitive-behavioral therapy, mindfulness, and setting realistic goals are some methods for overcoming perfectionism.

What are the signs that I'm a perfectionist?

Five Indications You May Be a Perfectionist and How to Find Harmony

While there are benefits to perfectionism, you should be careful that it hasn't become harmful.

Do you think of yourself as a stickler for detail? A few of us have an unending pursuit of perfection. This might seem honorable at its best, particularly if you are making progress in your goals. At your lowest point, however, you can have severe emotions of inadequacy, which might cause worry and low self-esteem.

So how can you strike a balance between the need for compassion and self-care and an ambition for success driven by perfectionism?

Perfectionism: What is it?

The pursuit of flawlessness is known as perfectionism, and it may be used to characterize a person's attitude toward life and their response to problems and obstacles.

Although it's not a recognized medical condition, many individuals may exhibit this prevalent personality feature. "Having very high and exact expectations and standards means that you are a perfectionist." "It involves working and making an effort to get things just so, or just right."

A lot of individuals develop perfectionism from an early age. Parents and other authoritative figures in our lives often affect how we see our values. Maybe you were raised to believe that you weren't accomplishing enough because of your perfectionism. Perhaps your parents encouraged you to constantly strive to be the greatest version of yourself, even if they didn't mean it.

Although this may foster ambition and excellent self-discipline, an excessive pursuit of perfection can also be harmful if it causes you to believe that your value is contingent upon your achievements.

Telltale signs of a potential perfectionist

Even while there may not be a definitive diagnosis for perfectionism, there are several telltale symptoms that might make you wonder whether you fall into this group.

The following characteristics are often linked to perfectionist behavior:

Your standards are very high.

It may indicate that you are a perfectionist if you aim for 150% success rather than merely 100% in all you do. Furthermore, you could place pressure on yourself to live up to those lofty expectations.

Put another way, a lot of the time, your standards serve as your compass. It's possible that you feel uneasy or that you need to make adjustments if things aren't going as planned or as expected.

Structure and order are what you thrive on.

Another indication of perfectionism is the need for ongoing order and structure. Someone who is highly particular about neatness and cleanliness, such as someone who makes their bed every morning or keeps their desk clear, might be an example of this.

A perfectionist will aim for that structure to consistently meet their standards, above and beyond mere organization.

You have extremely high expectations for yourself. Setting high standards has advantages. It may assist individuals in honing their abilities, even though nobody ever really gets flawless.

One benefit of perfectionism is that it often results in highly driven and hardworking individuals. They never give up. They never stop striving to improve things.

For example, perfectionism inclinations are frequent among artists, sportsmen, and even physicians. Because these professions often call for a high level of dedication and self-control, it makes sense that those who pursue them would always be looking for better.

You find it hard to get beyond minor errors. Persistently being too conscious of every error you've ever made, particularly in comparison to others around you, may also be an indication of perfectionism. Once again, acknowledging one's faults might be beneficial. However, stress may result from it when it's too severe.

You tend to put things off.
Perfectionism often results in procrastination. This may come as a surprise since you may assume that someone who is a perfectionist is constantly on top of things, but in many situations, perfectionism can contribute to procrastination.

This is due to the possibility that you will start to focus more on the outcome of your work than the actual process. Overemphasizing the outcome in the future might cause anxiety and perhaps make you ignore the current work.

Excessive perfectionism may make a job seem very difficult and produce a great deal of tension or worry. This dread of starting might set off a chain reaction of avoidance. "And then, finishing this task feels unachievable."

When the pursuit of perfection becomes detrimental
The effects of perfectionism may be considerably more harmful for certain people. However, how can you tell whether your perfectionism is going too far? The secret is to make an effort to understand who you are and take note of your reactions.

One drawback is that it often seems as if there is never enough, that there is perpetual unhappiness, a sense of not being good enough, and that one never really finds pleasure or satisfaction in what they have done.

Excessive perfectionism may harm you in the following ways:

Little regard for oneself: You generally don't need to worry if your perfectionism is showing out in more constructive ways, such as when you set high standards for yourself or gently push yourself to do better. However, the secret is to be aware of your personality and to see the signs that your perfectionist inclinations are leading you down a path of self-defeating thoughts and poor self-worth.

Mental health conditions: Perfectionist inclinations often coexist with, or even contribute to, mental health issues including social anxiety, eating disorders, and obsessive-compulsive disorder. Toxic perfectionism in this situation might exacerbate your mental health problems by acting as gasoline on the fire.

Connections: Furthermore, since you can always have unrealistic expectations for your relationships, this might also have an impact on how you connect with the people in your life. Your relationships may be beginning to suffer as a result of your perfectionism, which is something to be concerned about. "You will always be let down if you expect yourself or other people to be flawless."

Severe avoidance of tasks: To some extent, putting off a chore now and then is common. However, this may also be a warning sign if your perfectionism is keeping you from moving ahead in your life in several areas. Furthermore, perfectionism may be deterring you rather than encouraging you if it makes it difficult for you to do daily activities or leads you to adopt a scarcity mentality.

How to handle the need for perfection

Finding some coping mechanisms to help you achieve balance can be a good idea if you're realizing that your perfectionism is acting more like a burden and less like a driving force.

If you're goal-oriented, you need to discover the ideal balance between being motivated (and productive) and not torturing yourself.

Accept modesty: The first step is acknowledging that perfection is an unachievable objective, which won't be simple at first. Like everyone else, you will sometimes err, fail, or humiliate yourself. Accepting this idea may be very freeing.

Give yourself reasonable deadlines: Establishing reasonable deadlines can enable you to complete tasks at a more leisurely pace, whether they are personal, professional, or school-related. Setting deadlines might also assist you in learning to accept "good enough" work in the end rather than always aiming for excellence.

Learn to be able to laugh at oneself: While it's necessary to treat your responsibilities in life—such as job or school—seriously, you shouldn't allow them to negatively affect your feelings. Never forget to treat yourself with compassion and not take yourself too seriously.

Observe your resilience in the face of errors: You can probably recall some rather major mistakes you've made, as everyone can. Even though these circumstances were upsetting at the time, you managed to go through them. You could have even learned something.

Compare the advantages of aiming for perfection with the expenses: You could discover that the expenses are more than you anticipated: low self-esteem, difficulty unwinding, unwillingness to try new things, and persistent self-blame, for instance. Accepting that you are a messy, flawed person at times is very liberating.

Try purposefully creating something that isn't flawless

A small amount of clutter might sometimes be beneficial. Whether it's in your daily routine or the way your house is decorated, always remember to leave some space for spontaneity and the unexpected. Toxic perfectionism loses its grip on you when you learn to tolerate these very little flaws.

When to Get Assistance

If your perfectionism is beginning to interfere with your daily life, sleep habits, or sense of self-worth, it can be more detrimental than beneficial. Your mental health may suffer, for instance, if your perfectionism prevents you from trying new activities or negatively affects your mood.

Some folks may benefit from the assistance of a specialist. A therapist can help you feel accepted for who you are and identify any unfavorable messages you may be sending yourself if your perfectionism propensity is having a big negative influence on your life. Ultimately, you can develop self-compassion.

Chapter on Perfectionism

• Perfectionism is the pursuit of flawlessness in life.

• Unchecked perfectionism can lead to feelings of inadequacy and low self-esteem.

• Signs of perfectionism include setting high standards, thriving on structure, high expectations, overly critical of minor errors, and procrastination.

• Excessive perfectionism can negatively impact self-esteem, mental health, relationships, and task completion.

• To manage perfectionism, accept imperfection, set reasonable deadlines, learn to laugh at oneself, observe resilience, and weigh costs and benefits.

• Intentionally creating something imperfect can help loosen the grip of toxic perfectionism.

• Seeking therapist assistance can help develop self-compassion and address harmful thought patterns.

Is depression a result of perfectionism?

How Perfectionism is Linked to Anxicty

Perfectionism might appear innocent at first glance. Most of us try to be our best selves every single day, after all. But in actuality, perfectionism may manifest as an excessive desire to steer clear of the blunders, failures, and faults that, let's face it, are inevitable in life. Perfectionism is associated with anxiety and other mental health conditions, including obsessive-compulsive disorder (OCD), even though it is not a psychiatric problem in and of itself. Discover the reasons for perfectionism, how it relates to anxiety, and the relationship between perfectionism and mental health by continuing to read.

Potential Reasons for Perfectionism

The American Academy of Pediatrics states that you could have a hardwired perfectionism. Furthermore, it seems that this innate characteristic affects how a person perceives the environment.

Rather than having a "growth" perspective, perfectionists typically have a "fixed" mindset. Individuals who have a growth mindset think they can learn new things and develop over time. They are thus more equipped to handle setbacks. They don't associate failure with their feeling of value. On the other hand, those with fixed mindsets think that individuals are born with innate skills and abilities. These people have very high expectations for themselves and make every effort to succeed. Consequently, failure may cause people to reevaluate who they are.

Typical Indications of Perfectionism

Being a perfectionist is not a given for someone with high expectations. To determine if a person is a perfectionist, mental health practitioners often consider the individual's whole behavior and cognitive patterns. They search for the following red flags:

- → Aiming to fulfill certain requirements
- → Order and neatness are necessary
- → Fear of errors
- → Easily offended by criticism
- → Self-deprecation

Additionally, perfectionists often have irrationally high expectations for their significant others or other loved ones.

Is Anxiety a Symptom of Perfectionism?

Perfectionism and anxiety often coexist, even though their precise connection is difficult to understand. Anxious individuals, for instance, often exhibit more perfectionistic characteristics than the general public, according to a meta-analysis that was published in the Journal of Clinical Psychology.

When someone performs below their unreasonably high expectations, perfectionism may cause a cascade of worried thoughts and emotions. They attribute a portion of their self-worth to their performance, which explains why. They often perform to extremes at work, either by having unreasonable expectations or by trying desperately to avoid failing.

Perfectionists often see the world and themselves in terms of extremes: success or failure, good or evil. Anxiety is increased by thinking in such an excessive way. It does not allow for errors or obstacles that are typical in daily life.

Because of this, perfectionists are more inclined to focus on their worries and exacerbate their worries when things go wrong.

Reducing the Need for Perfectionism

Many techniques exist to help control perfectionism. Perfectionists often lose themselves in the endless "what ifs" of the future, the many things that may go wrong. Dismissing these thoughts may help for a while, but for some individuals, doing so might put them in a loop where their brains keep coming back to these ideas.

The concept of exposure and response prevention, or E/RP, helps people identify their concerns and come to terms with the fact that uncertainty is a natural part of life. It might be beneficial to consciously choose to accept the potential of undesirable outcomes to redirect your attention and energy toward the things that you can control.

The Link Between Perfectionism and Mental Health
Numerous mental health issues, such as anxiety, OCD, eating disorders, and obsessive-compulsive disorder, have been linked via research to perfectionism. Thus, it seems that perfectionism hurts mental health. Because of this, professionals think that treating a person's perfectionist inclinations should also include their general mental health.

Exploring Perfectionism and Anxiety

• Perfectionism leads to excessive fear of mistakes and failures, contributing to anxiety and other mental health conditions.

• Reasons for perfectionism include a fixed mindset and a preference for innate abilities over growth and learning.

• Signs of perfectionism include aiming for specific standards, valuing order, fearing errors, and self-deprecation.

• Anxiety often coexists with perfectionism, with anxious individuals showing more perfectionistic tendencies.

• Techniques like exposure and response prevention can reduce perfectionism.

• Perfectionism is linked to mental health issues like anxiety, OCD, eating disorders, and obsessive-compulsive disorder.

Is perfectionism a virtue or a vice?

The desire to seem, feel, and be flawless is known as perfectionism. Perfectionism may have harmful implications even though society often sees it as a favorable trait.

"Excessively high personal standards and overly critical self-evaluations" are characteristics of perfectionists.1. They want flawlessness and would settle for nothing less. This might show itself as efforts to control people and circumstances, as well as criticism of oneself and others.

An obsession with perfection

This episode of The Verywell Mind Podcast, hosted by therapist Amy Morin, LCSW, and featuring Peloton instructor Ally Love, explains how to prioritize progress over perfection.

Indications of an Idealistic Mindset

It's likely that you are, at least in part, a perfectionist if you're wondering whether you are. Because the term "perfect" has positive connotations, there's also a strong probability you have an interest in being a perfectionist.

High achievers and perfectionists are similar, although they vary greatly in several important ways. In this section, we discuss the variations and disclose 10 distinct indicators of a perfectionist, which you may be able to identify in yourself or someone you know.

All-or-Nothing Thinking: High achievers and perfectionists alike establish and strive toward very high standards. A perfectionist will accept nothing less than perfection, but a high achiever may be content with doing a fantastic job and reaching excellence (or something near) even if their objectives aren't fully accomplished. One views "almost perfect" as a failure.

How to Get Rid of the All-Or-Nothing Mentality

Being Extremely Skeptical

A perfectionist is more likely to be critical of others as well as oneself than a high achiever. High achievers are often supportive of others and take pleasure in their achievements, while perfectionists are quick to point out flaws.

A perfectionist will focus only on flaws and find it difficult to perceive anything else. When "failure" does happen, they are harder on themselves and others and more critical of them.

Being Pressed By Fear
High achievers are often drawn to their objectives by a strong desire to fulfill them. They are also pleased with any positive progress that has been accomplished. On the other side, perfectionists are often driven by a fear of failing to achieve their ideal.

Possessing Impractical Expectations
Setting unrealistic objectives is another indication that you are a perfectionist. High achievers can establish high standards for themselves and then take great pleasure in exceeding them. Perfectionists often set impossible beginning objectives for themselves.

A perfectionist often rejects accomplishment because they believe that their activities are never good enough to reach this level of performance since they have unrealistic expectations.

The Expectations vs. Reality Trap of Only Paying Attention to Outcomes

High achievers may take equal or more pleasure in the pursuit of a goal than in the objective's actual accomplishment. On the other hand, perfectionists only focus on the result. They are unable to appreciate the process of developing and striving because they are preoccupied with achieving the goal and avoiding failure.

Depression Resulting from Unmet Goals
High performers tend to be happier than perfectionists. When their high expectations aren't reached, perfectionists tend to beat themselves up and wallow in bad emotions, while high achievers can recover from disappointment very quickly. When things don't go as planned, they find it difficult to move on.

Perfectionists often experience lower levels of psychological well-being and greater degrees of anxiety in addition to lower levels of pleasure.

Fear of Not Getting Enough
Higher achievers are less afraid of failing than perfectionists. Failure becomes a frightening possibility because they get discouraged by anything less than perfection and put so much faith in outcomes. It is also hard to start something fresh since anything less than perfection is seen as a failure.

Good Strategies for Overcoming Failure and Procrastination

Given that procrastination may be damaging to productivity, it seems counterintuitive that perfectionists would also be prone to it. However, studies have shown that maladaptive perfectionism, or the inability of the perfectionist to adapt to their surroundings, makes them more likely to put things off.

The reason for this is that perfectionists, who dread failure, might get paralyzed with stress about doing something incorrectly and end up accomplishing nothing at all. A vicious and paralyzing cycle may be further perpetuated by this procrastination, which may subsequently result in increased feelings of failure.

Being defensive

Because they experience such agony and fear from a subpar performance, perfectionists often react negatively to helpful feedback. However, high performers might see criticism as useful knowledge that will help them do better in the future.

Poor Self-Regard

High performers often possess similar degrees of self-worth. Perfectionists are not like this. While the pursuit of perfectionism is linked to increased self-esteem, the critical self-evaluation that results from having a perfectionist disposition also lowers self-esteem.

Perfectionists' critical disposition and inflexibility, which drive people away, may also make them feel alone or alienated. This may result in even lower self-esteem, which might then negatively affect the person's relationships as well as their perception of themselves and their level of life satisfaction.

How to Handle Relationship Perfectionism

Reasons for Perfectionism

The likelihood of having a perfectionist personality may be influenced by a variety of things. Among the primary reasons for perfectionism are:

- → A dread of other people's opinions or judgment
- → Early life circumstances, such as having parents that set unreasonable standards for you
- → Possessing a mental health illness, such as obsessive-compulsive disorder (OCD), linked to perfectionist characteristics
- → Low self-worth
- → Sensations of insufficiency
- → A requirement for command
- → Equating success with one's value

The Dangers of Perfectionism

It's hard to be flawless or even to achieve a personal best, which makes being a perfectionist tough. One other issue with perfectionism, and the reason you should examine your perfectionistic tendencies, is that great achievers tend to accomplish more and experience less stress than perfectionists.

An unhealthy obsession with control is the hallmark of unhealthy perfectionism. Perfectionists tend to become highly particular and fixated on making sure everything is perfect, which may result in efforts to manipulate other people or circumstances. Interpersonal relationships may suffer as a result of this.

Additionally, it may be a factor in increased stress levels. Perfectionism-related stress has been connected to several detrimental effects, such as poor self-esteem, eating disorders, sleep difficulties, and psychological discomfort. It may also create anxiety.

Review

Reaching your objectives might be challenging if you suffer from unhealthy perfectionism. Negative consequences may include concern, tension, anxiety, and sadness.

How to Get Rid of Your Perfectionism

There are a few things you may take to lessen the harmful effects of your perfectionistic tendencies on your life. The following are some techniques to assist you get over your perfectionism:

- → Establishing a space where you feel welcomed
- → Having constructive self-talk
- → Avoiding making comparisons with other people
- → By engaging in mindfulness practices, you may learn to live more in the now and worry less about the past or the future.
- → Applying methods from cognitive behavioral therapy (CBT), such as questioning unfavorable ideas

While unhealthy perfectionism may result in worry, anxiety, poor self-esteem, and other problems that can lower one's quality of life, unhealthy perfectionism can motivate individuals to give their best effort. Perfectionists often have high standards, and are fear-driven, judgmental, and defensive in the face of criticism.

Don't give up if you recognize any of these perfectionist tendencies in yourself. Realizing that a change could be necessary is a crucial first step. As soon as you realize that these habits could be adversely impacting you, you can start working toward adopting a better strategy that will still enable you to accomplish your objectives with less anxiety and negativity.

Chapter Summary

Understanding Perfectionism

• Perfectionism is a trait characterized by high personal standards and critical self-evaluations.
• Indications include all-or-nothing thinking, extreme skepticism, fear, unrealistic expectations, and focus on outcomes.
• Reasons for perfectionism include fear of judgment, early life circumstances, mental health issues, low self-worth, need for control, and equating success with value.
• Dangers include increased stress, interpersonal relationship difficulties, poor self-esteem, eating disorders, sleep problems, psychological discomfort, anxiety, and sadness.
• Overcoming perfectionism involves creating a welcoming environment, engaging in constructive self-talk, avoiding comparisons, practicing mindfulness, and using CBT techniques.

Do those who strive for perfection find happiness?

Your Best Life: Perfectionism—The Bane of Happiness

Aspiring people often refer to themselves as "perfectionists," and many even take pride in this designation. Giving perfectionism a good spin might mask deeper, more serious problems. Perfectionism and the "pursuit of excellence" must be distinguished from one another. Rather than perfectionism, working hard or going above and beyond to accomplish a goal is a show of dedication. Perfectionism often stems from worry or problems with self-worth, which have been connected to lower levels of personal satisfaction and a higher risk of suicide.

Eating disorders, anxiety disorders, and depression are indeed more common among perfectionists. One lives in constant terror and great care in such a life. When perfection is the only choice, creativity, pleasure, inspiration, and even productivity are stifled. Ironically, successful individuals are less likely to be perfectionists, according to Flett and colleagues, since perfectionism's symptoms tend to impede one's ability to reach greater levels of achievement.

A lot of us strive for excellence. Even while we secretly know that perfection is unattainable, we nonetheless make an effort to execute flawless medical operations and to foster—or at the very least, project—perfect marriages. However, we've all heard stories of surgeons wasting almost six hours in the operating room trying to accomplish the "perfect" fracture reduction in a procedure that normally takes much less time.

Perfectionism may drain a surgeon's vitality in a field as demanding as orthopedic surgery, leaving little time for relationships and self-care. The surgeon may decide to postpone difficult situations. Patients who are easily managed by an average surgeon on any given day are often sent to other facilities.

To put it simply, perfectionists are afraid of flaws and believe that every mistake indicates a personal shortcoming. In general, perfectionists are quite sensitive to criticism. They put off doing things, waiting for the ideal opportunity. A perfectionist never feels joy in their accomplishments, even when they succeed. Rather, relief that they succeeded this time around prevails. They go about their lives believing that the only way to accept oneself is to achieve perfection.

The History of Perfectionism

Perfectionism often masks a problem with self-worth. A key caregiver—typically a parent—likely sent the perfectionist signals of conditional approval throughout their formative years. It was obvious what the message meant: "I will love you if..." A child's injured self-image might be shaped by a parent's expectations for them to be ideal in their conduct, academic performance, or athletics. A predisposition toward neuroticism and the existence of domineering and cold-hearted parental figures have been identified as typical characteristics in the upbringing of perfectionists. The load of intrusive thoughts that each of us faces is mostly determined by our upbringing and hereditary factors. If abnormal thinking patterns are not identified and treated, the pressure to perform creates intrusive ideas in the young person's head that will persist throughout their life.

Disturbances in Thinking

Perfectionism is a result of cognitive problems. Cognitive behavioral scientists have classified incorrect, erroneous thought processes into several cognitive distortions. Every "cognitive distortion" is just a deception that our brains tell our conscious minds. One common distortion is to focus on the negative parts of an event rather than its good features, which causes one's mind to get overtaken by ideas of all that is wrong with it. It's a typical case of focusing on the negative rather than the good when there is one misplaced screw in an otherwise excellent fracture reduction.

All-or-nothing thinking is another cognitive error that perfectionists often exhibit. In other words, a single unfavorable experience might set off a chain reaction of bothersome ideas that extrapolate bad luck into every area of a person's life. For example, a perfectionist may have a wave of negative thoughts after a difficult operation, such as "I am no good," "I am a lousy surgeon," or even "I don't deserve to be called doctor."

Perfectionists are also more likely to personalize and assign blame, which is the inclination to hold oneself accountable for actions that one did not fully commit. Another is labeling, which is the tendency for someone to build their whole identity around their flaws. Rather than owning up to their errors, labelers are eager to call themselves "losers" or utter failures. Up to ten frequent cognitive distortions may be experienced by perfectionists, and they all contribute to a decrease in their level of pleasure and satisfaction.

The Will to Embrace Imperfections

The first step towards rehabilitation is realizing and acknowledging these false beliefs. Correcting incorrect thought patterns is necessary for recovery from perfection. Make room for perfectionistic ideas. Just take a deep breath and let these bothersome ideas go when they emerge. Realize that the emotions and feelings that motivate you to strive for perfection are delusions your mind is feeding you. You should see the compulsions and neurotic behaviors that resulted from your perfectionistic beliefs as nothing more than mental tricks. See our earlier piece about mindfulness, or being present in the moment. Becoming fully present causes our obsessive and intrusive thoughts to lessen. Our ability to manage our thoughts will greatly improve from everyday practice, as well as by reading books and taking mindfulness classes.

Thomas S. Greenspon, Ph., a psychologist, and marital and family therapist, suggested "building an environment of acceptance" in his 2008 research by using discussion, empathy, self-reflection, and encouragement. According to Greenspon, these are the foundations of a method that will assist someone in getting over perfectionism-related beliefs rather than actual processes.

According to this perspective, perfectionism stems from emotional beliefs about what it takes to be accepted as a person, as stated by Greenspon in the research. It's not just a collection of illogical ideas that may be disproved by choosing to adopt a different perspective; rather, it represents the fundamental understanding of reality held by a perfectionist. Perfectionism is a protection when there is so much emotion at risk. It takes time and effort to overcome perfectionism; it's more like fostering a flower's blossoming than mending a damaged item.

Beyond Greenspon's perspective, treatment may be obtained with a therapist; cognitive behavioral therapy has shown to be particularly successful in this regard. A qualified therapist may assist in dissecting and reframing ideas that cause worry and anxiety into more grounded ideas. Additionally, finding a mentor who has the ideal ratio of acceptance to self-compassion may be a very powerful pattern for one's life. We may learn to be more accepting of ourselves if we see that others would embrace us more completely when we are genuine rather than a "perfect" pseudo self that our brains have created out of fear.

Visit Here to Try This Tomorrow
For the next thirty days, "Dare to be average," in the words of David Burns, MD. Recognize your imperfections and fight the urge to succumb to fear.

Simply exist and get in touch with your creative side. Instead of thinking about what you ought to be doing, let inspiration and passion take over.

Write out the benefits and drawbacks of your perfectionism. Using this activity, Burns tries to persuade his patients that when perfectionism sets in, their productivity suffers.

Being more **"process-oriented"** as opposed to **"results-oriented"** is another strategy that is suggested. For instance, let go of the need to do the ideal operation and concentrate on making a strong, continuous effort in the operating room. The establishment of reasonable time constraints for every activity is implicit in a process-oriented approach. Make sure you follow them. The increase in productivity and level of enjoyment you experience will surprise you.

Consider errors as chances for improvement as opposed to indications of failure. Errors are where we learn, not triumphs. Every seeming step backward just moves us one step closer to our objectives.

Distinguishing Perfectionism from Pursuit of Excellence

• Perfectionism stems from self-worth issues, leading to lower personal satisfaction and higher risk of mental health issues.

• It stifles creativity, pleasure, inspiration, and productivity, hindering success.

• Perfectionism often masks a problem with self-worth influenced by upbringing and cognitive distortions.

• Rehabilitation from perfectionism involves acknowledging false beliefs, correcting incorrect thought patterns, practicing mindfulness, and creating an acceptance environment.

• Treatment options include cognitive behavioral therapy and finding mentors.

• Overcoming perfectionism involves daring to be average, focusing on the process, setting time constraints, and viewing errors as opportunities for improvement.

Why should you give up trying to be perfect?

Perfectionists believe that aiming for perfection is a positive thing to do and that settling for anything less would ruin the impression they wish to make.

And because most people in our culture strive to hold themselves to a high level, this is often seen as a virtue. It is seen as a positive personality attribute and a sign of a strong work ethic.

We've all been encouraged since we were little children to strive for excellence in whatever we do, and if we don't, there's no point in doing it at all.

Like you, I was raised to believe that we should all strive for perfectionism and that there is nothing wrong with it.

Before, I didn't see anything wrong with those who brag about how meticulous and precise they are about everything. However, I have seen a lot of people make these claims.

But after over ten years, I no longer genuinely think that perfectionism exists, and I no longer aim for perfection.

This is because I realized that my previous attempts to aim for perfection were ineffective. And these are the whole list of causes:

Reasons to give up on becoming perfect

1. Perfectionism prevents you from taking on new endeavors.
You don't allow yourself to start anything fresh because you won't settle for anything less than perfection. Any new endeavor will always need you to start from scratch.

First things are typically untidy. It is impossible to be flawless right from the start since beginnings are inherently flawed. No one can.

Because they just cannot handle not being flawless from the beginning, perfectionists never start anything new and, if they do, seldom have the confidence to finish.

In the second episode of my podcast, "The Heart of Living," I discussed my own experience of battling perfectionism.

I thought that if I couldn't do anything flawlessly, I shouldn't do it at all, therefore I would continually compare myself to the best.

I see that a lot of us have this inclination to believe that we must be flawless right away.

However, you have to be aware of this propensity toward perfectionism that leads you to believe that you have to be flawless right away.

Perfectionism may seem noble, but in reality, it prevents us from taking risks and failing to take any action at all.

2. You become overly harsh on yourself due to perfectionism
Sly is perfectionism. You unintentionally beat yourself up and become too hard on yourself, but it gives you the impression that it is noble and that you are doing your hardest when you strive to be flawless.

When you want to be flawless, you deny yourself the opportunity to learn from your errors and feel guilty about being unprofessional. Additionally, no matter how hard you work, you may believe that your efforts are insufficient.

When the outcome still doesn't please you, you then tend to labor until you burn out.

This either convinces you to give up completely on your endeavors or to believe that you will never be the greatest.

You begin comparing yourself to others without realizing that the greatest people also had a period when they were only okay.

3. The need for perfection prevents you from making errors
"You are never allowed to make mistakes," perfectionism asserts, and when you do, it makes you feel as if you have made the worst error possible.

You must let go of your obsession with perfection because you will never grow without allowing yourself to make errors and grow from them.

If you make even the smallest error, perfectionism may lead to negative self-talk in the following ways;

> *You're awful.*
> *You don't have the self-control to communicate this and you are nothing.*

Everyone will condemn you; you'll never be like them; you have no skill; you'll never be good at this; you have no authority to share this; and the list goes on and on.

All I'm trying to express here is that you have to allow yourself to make errors.

Making errors is a sign of trying, therefore I hope you make a lot of them.

Additionally, making an effort and persevering is more morally admirable than wanting everything to be flawless and giving up altogether.

4. Perfectionism prevents you from appreciating the experience
You get too fixated on the outcome because you are overly preoccupied with having and doing everything perfectly.

You fear making any kind of mistake.

Because of this, perfectionists are gloomy and never seem to enjoy the trip.

When you find yourself too fixated on the outcome and angry that it's taking too long to happen, take a step back and consider if your perfectionist inclinations are to blame.

The true reason you want things to go flawlessly quickly and you don't want to make any errors at all is because you want to see the actual results quickly and seem to be the greatest in front of others quickly.

But that's a certain way to increase stress, worry, and mental burden.

Instead, just let go and permit yourself to walk gently.

Allow yourself to make errors; in fact, picture yourself as embarking on an amazing trip in which you will learn from your blunders, confront your limiting beliefs, and discover what happens when you don't give up. Just allow yourself enough room to notice how each day's steps are advancing you.

When you eventually get at your goal and realize how far you've come from where you were, this will make you feel amazing.

5. Having a perfectionist mindset causes you to worry excessively about criticism.

Additionally, perfectionism gives us the impression that we are all to blame for everyone's judgment of us if we are not flawless.

We believe that if we pay close attention to every detail and strive for perfection in every one of them, then no one will be able to criticize us.

But if there's one thing I've learned about creativity and work, it's that our job is to do tasks to the best of our knowledge and abilities at the moment, regardless of what other people may think.

There will always be someone to talk to. Our task is to do our job as efficiently as possible while using as little pressure as possible.

As Maya Angelou puts it, "Until you know better, do the best you can." Then act better once you are aware of this. Give off worrying so much about criticism.

It is none of your concern how other people see you. It is your business to follow your passions and do as you like.

There will always be the dread of judgment. Allow it to exist, but resist letting it overcome you.

Give up trying to please everyone and learn to accept criticism instead.

You just carry out the tasks for which you were sent here. Here are my arguments on why you should give up being a perfectionist and why it's not anything to be proud of.

Why being a perfectionist is unhealthy and why we shouldn't be one

What happens if you give up trying to be perfect? The majority of us believe that if we don't strive for perfection, we will produce substandard work or fail to leave our greatest impression on the world, but this isn't the case.

You permit yourself to begin before you feel prepared.

Indeed, you'll never feel prepared. You begin in any case by not striving for flawlessness. This method of approaching procrastination is effective since perfectionism is a major contributing factor to procrastination.

You allow yourself to make errors and pick things up gradually.

All you have to do is concentrate on doing your task as efficiently as possible at that particular moment.

You begin to have greater faith in yourself.

Your flexibility increases significantly.

You become considerably more self-compassionate.

You get burned out and quit working.

You begin to value who you are and all that you have accomplished.

You give up worrying about what others think of you.

Instead of cheering for the outcome, you begin to appreciate the process.

Why I no longer strive for perfection

I am no longer supporting perfectionism and have broken up with it.

This is what has enabled me to continue on my blogging adventure and to stay motivated.

Even with blogging and writing, at first, I was putting too much pressure on myself and trying to be flawless.

Nevertheless, over time, I overcame this perfectionist tendency and now I just view the entire process as an experiment, a learning process, and a way to see what would happen if I didn't give up.

My little site now has over 200k monthly visitors, and I make an effort to focus on simplicity rather than perfection.

If I had begun earlier, I never would have done any of it because I would have been too worried about not knowing enough and not being good enough.

I know it will be freeing for you too, but for me, breaking free from perfectionism has been liberating.
I hope that instead of worrying about perfection, we simply keep doing the best we can with what we know and let ourselves go gently on our path.

"Drawbacks of Perfectionism"

• Prevents new ventures: Perfectionism can deter individuals from starting new projects due to fear of not being flawless.

• Harsh Self-Criticism: Perfectionists often overly criticize themselves, leading to feelings of inadequacy and burnout.

• Fear of Making Mistakes: Perfectionism instills a fear of making mistakes, inhibiting growth and learning.

• Inability to Enjoy the Process: Perfectionists focus too much on the outcome, leading to increased stress and dissatisfaction.

• Excessive Worry About Criticism: Perfectionists worry excessively about others' perception, leading to anxiety and fear of judgment.

• Benefits of Overcoming Perfectionism: Increased self-compassion, flexibility, and enjoyment of the process.

Do perfectionists overthink things?

8 Unexpected Reasons Why Perfectionism Is Bad for Your Mental Health

Perfectionism is often commended for enabling us to focus on the finer points and strive for excellence. However, there are also major drawbacks to this feature, which is sometimes seen positively and may have a big effect on your mental health. This post will highlight these neglected problems and provide helpful advice on how to resolve them. Perfectionism may lead to tension, worry, and even melancholy behind the surface of immaculate work and high expectations. We want to provide you with a more rounded perspective by delving into the less discussed effects, enabling you to make better decisions for your health.

To comprehend how perfectionism may cause or exacerbate a variety of mental health issues, it is important to grasp what perfectionism entails. Perfectionism is often connected to anxiety, despair, and in some cases, obsessive-compulsive disorder (OCD). Discover precisely how perfectionism may harm your mental health as well as some strategies for overcoming it by reading on.

Perfectionism Is Bad for Your Mental Health for These 8 Reasons:

1. Captured in Overanalyzing
Pursuing perfection may often lead to an overthinking spiral. You become stuck and start thinking about the "what ifs" and worst-case situations all the time. You may be unable to make choices, fulfill deadlines, and ultimately experience an increase in stress and worry as a result of this paralysis.

Use strategies like mindfulness or segmenting your work into manageable portions. These techniques may assist you in overcoming the barrier that overthinking erects.

2. The Danger of Self-Comparison with Others
A lot of perfectionists use other people's opinions of them to determine their value. They prioritize the accomplishments and possessions of others above their

special talents. This may cause negative self-esteem, detrimental feelings of inadequacy, and even the onset of social anxiety.

Practical Advice: Keep your attention on your path by starting a daily thankfulness routine or keeping a "win journal" to track your achievements.

3. A fear of making mistakes

For perfectionists, the fear of failing is a constant concern. They see failure as disastrous, something that diminishes their worth as individuals. In addition to causing stress, this intense worry may exacerbate more serious illnesses like generalized anxiety disorder.

Practical Advice: Use cognitive restructuring strategies to reframe failure as an opportunity for learning rather than a catastrophic event that will change your life.

4. Relationship Stress

Relationships may be ruined by perfectionism. It creates needless conflict between friends and family members and establishes unreasonable expectations for relationships. Disappointment cycles, social anxiety, and even obsessive-compulsive behaviors may result from it.

Practical Advice: Try to build genuine relationships rather than flawless ones and be honest with your loved ones about your perfectionism inclinations.

5. Postponing tasks due to perfectionism
Ironically, striving for perfection might make you put things off. You put off beginning initiatives because you think the end product won't live up to your lofty expectations. This delay raises your stress levels and may be a factor in sadness or feelings of inadequacy.

Use the "two-minute rule" to jumpstart tiny chores to create a snowball effect that will make larger jobs easier to take on. This is practical advice.

6. Having unpleasant physical symptoms
Perfectionism causes tension that goes beyond your mind. It often takes physical form. Common symptoms like insomnia and tension headaches lead to a vicious cycle that deteriorates your mental health even further.

Practical Advice: To reduce stress, make regular exercise, yoga, or relaxation exercises like deep breathing a part of your daily routine.

7. Disregarding Your Needs for Emotions
It's easy to overlook your emotional requirements while you're chasing perfection. Chronic mental health issues

like sadness or anxiety are a result of this lack of emotional self-care.

Realistic Suggestion: Give emotional well-being a priority. For more formal help, schedule frequent emotional check-ins or participate in talking therapy.

8. Locked within a Fixed Mental Model
Perfectionism may put you in a strict frame of mind that makes it difficult to grow or adjust to new situations. This rigidity hinders your ability to develop personally and lowers your level of life happiness, which exacerbates mental health issues.

Practical Advice: To overcome the rigidity that perfectionism often brings, adopt a development attitude. Consider obstacles as chances to grow and learn.

Counseling: An Approach to Handle Perfectionism
Self-help techniques are a terrific place to start, but in certain cases, perfectionism has deep roots that call for expert advice to make a significant difference. A secure environment to examine the underlying problems that underlie your perfectionistic inclinations may be provided via therapy.

For instance, cognitive behavioral therapy (CBT) assists in identifying and substituting healthy beliefs for thinking patterns that support perfectionism. Acceptance and Commitment Therapy (ACT), which teaches you to accept mistakes and commit to behaviors that are consistent with your beliefs instead of aiming for unachievable standards, is another helpful strategy. Some find solace in group therapy, where it may be very illuminating to share experiences and coping mechanisms with others going through comparable struggles.

Consider consulting with a licensed therapist if your mental health is suffering as a result of perfectionism. They may customize the course of therapy to meet your requirements, guiding you in setting reasonable objectives and offering support through the highs and lows of letting go of perfectionism.

Although perfectionism may seem positive at first, it is often the underlying cause of several mental health problems. Being aware of these drawbacks will enable you to mitigate their effects. It's OK to be imperfect; in fact, it's better for you.

Importance of Overcoming Perfectionism's Impact on Mental Health

• Overanalyzing: Perfectionism can lead to paralysis, hindering decision-making and increasing stress. Strategies like mindfulness and task breaks can help.

• Self-Comparison: Perfectionism often leads to negative self-esteem and social anxiety. Practices like gratitude journaling can help focus on personal achievements.

• Fear of Failure: Perfectionism can cause stress and anxiety by viewing failure as a learning opportunity. Cognitive restructuring techniques can help reframe failure.

• Relationship Stress: Perfectionism can strain relationships by creating unrealistic expectations and conflict. Building genuine connections and honesty about perfectionist tendencies can alleviate relationship stress.

• Procrastination: Techniques like the "two-minute rule" can help overcome procrastination.

• Physical Symptoms: Regular exercise and relaxation techniques can help reduce physical symptoms.

• Neglecting Emotional Needs: Prioritizing emotional self-care through check-ins or therapy can help address this.

• Rigidity: Perfectionism creates a fixed mindset hindering personal growth and happiness.

• Seeking therapy can provide a supportive environment for exploring underlying issues and developing coping strategies.

Can one overcome perfectionism?

10 Ways to Overcome Perfectionism

Being a high achiever and being a perfectionist are two different things. People of both kinds aspire to success. High achievers, on the other hand, are driven to strive for excellence, but perfectionists are driven by fear and immobilized by the thought of failing. Here are some crucial facts regarding perfectionism to be aware of before we talk about how to get over it:

Because perfectionism may cause extreme stress, dread of being judged, or feelings of inadequacy, it can negatively impact our sense of calm, pleasure in life, and self-worth.

Perfectionism-related traits are often connected to mental health conditions including stress, anxiety, and OCD.

Perfectionists put pressure on themselves to live up to unrealistic expectations. They are very hard on themselves and punish anything that doesn't live up to their expectations.

Perfectionists also worry that if they don't aim for excellence, they won't accomplish their objectives and will instead become poor performers. When a perfectionist's dread of failing overwhelms them, they may put off doing something altogether rather than risk failing miserably. When we fall victim to the perfectionist myth and have unreasonable expectations of others around us, we hurt other people.

How to Get Rid of Perfectionism:

1. Recognize Your Predispositions More
Being conscious of your perfectionist thoughts and behaviors is the first step towards conquering perfectionism. Pause for a moment and observe how you think about perfectionism. To help you better comprehend these ideas, you may even attempt to put them in writing. We can change the way we communicate to ourselves about perfectionism once we recognize the ways it creeps into our lives.

2. Pay Attention to the Good

When we strive for perfection, we often get fixated on the flaws in our work or ourselves. But it's crucial that we consciously work to see the positive things as well. Try to think of three things that you do enjoy for every item that you're not quite content with.

3. Permit yourself to make errors

When we permit ourselves to make errors, we may realize that failing is not fatal. We have the chance to improve, learn from, and grow from our mistakes. Taking up a new pastime that you probably won't be excellent at on your first attempt is one approach to practice this. Consider enjoying the activity and gradually improving rather than striving to be "perfect" at it. You may discover that making errors is an essential part of the process to reach your goals.

4. Make More Reasonable Objectives

Perfectionists sometimes have unachievable standards, which leads them to establish unreasonable goals. Setting more realistic, SMART objectives is one method to overcome perfectionism. When our objectives are reasonable and somewhat hard, we will feel much less stressed and more certain of our ability to achieve them.

5. Acquire The Ability to Take Criticism.
Because they take criticism personally, perfectionists often have poor self-esteem. On the other hand, it's important to receive constructive criticism so that we can improve. Try to understand that constructive criticism is natural and may be useful in helping us become better. Errors or mishaps are quite typical on the journey.

6. Lessen the Self-Pressure You Apply
Never forget that you are the one putting the greatest strain on yourself. Lower the impossible expectations you set for yourself and be kind to yourself. This will help you to learn to accept who you are. You're doing well as long as you're still driven and giving it your all. While being "perfect" does not exist, we may take pride in having tried our hardest.

7- Give Meaning More Weight Than Perfection
Instead of concentrating on doing things flawlessly, attempt to change your attention to discover significance in what you do. Whether anything is done properly or not doesn't matter as long as it fulfills us and gives us pleasure. Finding significance along the journey might lead to greater satisfaction.

8- Try Not to Put Things Off
Perfectionists are often infamous procrastinators who use their inability to guarantee perfection as an excuse to put

off doing their tasks. In the long term, this may be much more stressful and counterproductive. Starting is often the toughest part, but even just outlining our task in rudimentary form in advance is preferable to doing nothing at all. Remind yourself that it's OK if your first attempt or draft isn't flawless, and allow yourself the opportunity to continue working on the project.

9- Eliminate Adverse Influences

We must keep an eye on how media such as podcasts, novels, movies, TV shows, and social media may promote perfectionism. Social media's promotion of a narrative of "hustle culture" and perfectionism in our profession should particularly concern us. Reducing or eliminating these channels may also assist us in letting go of our perfectionism.

10. See a therapist

Finally, therapy may alleviate our perfectionism-related anxiety. In particular, cognitive behavioral therapy (CBT) may assist sufferers of perfectionism in reframing their ideas. You may have a deeper understanding of the underlying cause of the pressure to be flawless via therapy. Therapy might be an excellent choice if you discover that you're still having trouble overcoming your perfectionism.

Overcoming Perfectionism Strategies

• Recognize Perfectionist Tendencies: Acknowledge and acknowledge when perfectionism arises.

• Balance Critical Thoughts with Positives: Balance critical thoughts with positive ones.

• Allow Mistakes: Embrace mistakes as learning opportunities.

• Set Realistic Goals: Avoid unattainable standards and set SMART goals.

• Learn to Accept Criticism: Separate feedback from personal worth.

• Reduce Self-Imposed Pressure: Be kind to yourself and lower unrealistic expectations.

• Focus on Meaning Over Perfection: Shift focus from perfection to finding fulfillment.

• Avoid Procrastination: Start tasks even if they won't be perfect.

• Limit Negative Influences: Be mindful of media and societal pressures that promote perfectionism.

• Seek Therapy: Consider cognitive behavioral therapy or other forms of therapy.

Is perfectionism a genetic trait?

Perfectionism is a way of thinking and doing that is a mentality. It encompasses a wide range of behaviors, including being meticulous, aiming for excellence, having very high standards, finding it difficult to make choices, being afraid of failing, being intolerant of errors, and believing that we are not good enough and that we must work harder to live up to our high standards. Perfectionists often have high expectations for themselves and evaluate themselves harshly. Most significantly, perfectionism is a coping strategy used to deal with unpleasant ideas.

Perfectionism: What Is Its Cause?
However, how can we develop these self-critical ideas and ways of thinking? Indeed, we don't have these ideas from birth. In actuality, the experiences we encounter throughout life are what cause us to develop this overcompensating perfectionist mechanism. Because of

this, perfectionism is a traumatic reaction for a large number of individuals. Perfectionism, to put it simply, is a learned behavior that develops as a result of painful life events. The three most typical causes of perfectionism are discussed below:

Our Maternal Sources
First, we look at our parents, who are usually the first to detect trauma. But hold on, let's not accuse our parents right now. All we need to do is try to figure out how their actions affected our own. The majority of parents made an effort to the best of their abilities and the resources available to them at the time. Our parents struggled and had their frailties while attempting to raise us. When we were kids, we relied on them, wanted to be loved by them, and felt emotionally and psychologically secure until we made even the smallest mistake.

Being loved and nurtured was all we desired throughout our very sensitive formative years. If our parents were too demanding, overly ambitious, or high achievers while we were growing up, we probably turned to perfectionist tendencies as a coping mechanism. Because of this, one of the most frequent causes of perfectionism is these kinds of parenting approaches. However, how do these parents act?

A parent who is too ambitious is one who:
> *Concentrate on our errors and shortcomings,*
> *Test us to the utmost,*
> *Do not let us pause,*
> *Terrify us with the most dire failure scenarios,*
> *Neglect our wants and emotions,*

Concentrate only on your accomplishments

In severe situations, parents who mistreat, denigrate, and embarrass us may also penalize you for having failed at something or for not being the ideal kid.

If you grew up in a home like this, this is most likely where you first heard the expression "You disappointed me," which may have left you feeling deeply wounded. This is also most likely the first time you heard the phrase "What would people say," which lingered in your mind since it appears that other people's opinions matter more than your own or your parents'. These are the times when you experience intense disappointment along with worry, dread, fear, and tension related to your own identity. This turns into your first encounter with shame, an emotion strongly linked to perfectionism. It is because no one was present to console you or provide an explanation during these occurrences that they are referred to be trauma.

We resorted to developing the overcompensating mechanism of perfectionism to deal with this pain, humiliation, and embarrassment. Because of this, perfectionism may be a traumatized reaction. We attempt to cope with the guilt and internalized sense of deficiency we have about ourselves by engaging in perfectionism. This is the catalyst for the whispers in our heads that subtly remind us that we are never good enough and that we need to do more things to be liked and appreciated.

Bullying is another factor unrelated to our parents that contributes to perfectionism. Being raised by high achievers might have similar impacts to those of being bullied as a kid or teenager. When we were bullied, we were made to feel inadequate and embarrassed of who we were. We were led to believe that our appearance, our choices of clothing, our social circle, our musical tastes, and our academic standing were insufficient. This time, our classmates or even professors were the ones making these critiques.

However, once again, the only method we've discovered to deal with this deplorable "reality" is to constantly give it our all. There were moments when we even fantasized about the day we would prove to our bullies how strong we were. We used to fantasize that one day we would say things like, "One day I will be so important that nobody will ever doubt my worth, my value, and my importance," or "One day you will beg to be my friend." Furthermore, these ideas feed our need for perfection and perfectionism.

Transitions and Upsetting Occurrences

Lastly, stressful experiences or abrupt transitions we went through as kids may also contribute to perfectionism. These are the things that happened to rock our world when we were little. A family member passing away unexpectedly, relocating to a different nation, city, or school, or experiencing chaos inside the family are a few examples. A youngster may find all of these things to be quite overwhelming and will make a valiant effort to regain some control over their life. Hence, if a youngster is unable to regulate their surroundings, they will attempt to regulate their inner self, ideas, and reality. Here, striving for perfection is our last-ditch attempt at self-control and internal safety.

So, Is Anxiety Relating To Perfectionism?

When we were younger, perfectionism served as a coping strategy to help us get by and get through life. It was our way of reacting to an unreliable and unfriendly world. However, it is now backfiring. As we get older, we discover that we no longer need this coping strategy and that it is doing more damage than good. We have the resources available to us as adults to identify healthier coping mechanisms. We should focus on improving ourselves and how to grow as individuals. There may be moments when we want to attempt to modify our parents' perfectionist habits. But we have to keep in mind that this is our fight, not theirs. They may not even be conscious that they are perfectionists, nor that they are prepared for it or have had time to absorb their life experiences. All we have to do is recognize the origins of our inclinations, how we came to have this worldview, and, if necessary, establish boundaries with others around us.

Our experiences in life have taught us to respond to tragedy by becoming perfectionists. Right now, we want to work on our behaviors and self-talk. Our relationships may suffer as a result of perfectionism, which may even result in burnout. Therefore, if you think you may be a perfectionist, we encourage you to read our free guide to find out. After that, you may start the process of overcoming your traumas and using healthy coping mechanisms. But keep in mind that you are not alone—many others are also experiencing difficulties with perfectionism.

Causes and Impacts of Perfectionism

Causes:
• Parental Influence: High expectations and overly critical parenting styles can foster perfectionist tendencies.
• Bullying and Social Pressures: Experiences of bullying, social rejection, or feeling inadequate can fuel perfectionism.
• Traumatic Life Events: Significant life changes or traumatic experiences during childhood can trigger perfectionism as a coping mechanism.

Impacts:
• High Stress and Anxiety: Perfectionists often experience high stress and anxiety due to the pressure to meet unrealistic standards.
• Strained Relationships: Perfectionism can strain relationships, leading to conflict and dissatisfaction.
• Negative Self-Evaluation: Perfectionists may feel inadequacy or worthlessness if they fall short of their own expectations.

Addressing Perfectionism:

• Self-Awareness: Recognize perfectionist tendencies and understand their origins to develop self-compassion and empathy.

• Challenge Negative Thoughts: Replace self-critical thoughts with more realistic and compassionate perspectives.

• Set Realistic Goals: Establish achievable goals and focus on progress rather than perfection.

• Practice Self-Compassion: Treat oneself with kindness and understanding.

• Seek Support: Reach out to friends, family, or mental health professionals for support and guidance.

How do I get rid of my need for perfection?

The Perils of Trying to Be Perfect

At first glance, perfectionism could seem like a positive trait that promotes success and high accomplishment levels. But the reality is often far from ideal. Perfectionism may result in several problems, such as:

Procrastination: Perfectionists sometimes put off or forego beginning undertakings entirely out of the paralyzing dread of falling short of their irrational standards. This may impede development and lead to unneeded stress.

Burnout: In their quest for perfection, perfectionists often overwork themselves. This may result in emotional and physical tiredness, which might have detrimental effects on one's general health and well-being.

Perfectionism may cause problems in relationships with friends, family, and coworkers. The demand for control, critical nature, and exaggerated expectations of a perfectionist may lead to conflict and sour relations with others.

Diminished Creativity: Thinking outside the box and being afraid of failing are two things that might limit creativity. This may hinder someone's ability to develop, create, and adapt in a variety of spheres of life.

Low Self-Esteem: A perfectionist may have low self-worth and feelings of inadequacy when they fall short of their impossible standards.

Perfectionism and Mental Well-Being

Perfectionism may have a serious detrimental effect on mental health. Perfectionists often struggle with elevated stress, anxiety, and depressive symptoms. This may be brought on by a persistent sense of inadequacy, failure to live up to one's standards, and the conviction that one is never good enough.

Perfectionism's aftermath may lead to two of the main reasons for mental health problems:

Perfectionism and Anxiety

Perfectionism may exacerbate anxiety by inciting a never-ending loop of concern and ruminating. Perfectionists might be afraid of making errors, letting others down, or falling short of their standards. This may result in a persistent state of hyperarousal that is detrimental to their general and mental health.

Perfectionism and Depression

Perfectionists may experience emotions of pessimism and despair when they are unable to continuously live up to their own very high standards. This may worsen pre-existing depression or aid in the onset of depressed symptoms. One of the main risk factors for depression might be a persistent sense of inadequacy.

Strategies & Interventions for Getting Rid of Perfectionism

Finding balance in life and enhancing mental health requires acknowledging and resolving perfectionism. You may overcome perfectionism in a few different ways. Among them are:

→ *Cognitive Behavioral Therapy*
→ *Meditation and Mindfulness*

➜ Self-awareness;   realistic goal-setting
➜ Looking for assistance
➜ Getting a growth mentality
➜ Developing Resilience
➜ Getting expert assistance

Let's examine each strategy in more detail and see how it might assist you in overcoming perfectionism

Therapy based on cognitive behavior (CBT)
CBT is an empirically supported treatment that aims to recognize and address harmful thinking patterns and behaviors. Through the identification and modification of perfectionistic attitudes and beliefs, CBT may assist people in developing better-coping strategies and lowering their levels of anxiety and sadness.

Its methodical and goal-oriented approach enables people to create useful coping mechanisms and techniques for efficiently managing their symptoms. Additionally, CBT has shown to be a time-limited treatment, often producing fruitful outcomes in a very short amount of time when compared to some other therapeutic modalities. CBT is a cornerstone in the area of psychology and a useful tool for helping people recover control over their lives and enhance their general mental well-being because of its evidence-based design, which has been shown in multiple research.

Meditation and Mindfulness

People who meditate and practice mindfulness may become more aware of their thoughts, feelings, and physical sensations. They may be able to identify their perfectionistic inclinations and find more constructive strategies to deal with them thanks to their increased self-awareness.

With the help of mindfulness, people may notice their thoughts, feelings, and actions without passing judgment on them. This liberates them from the harsh self-criticism that perfectionists often place on themselves. People may learn to let go of the never-ending quest for perfection and become more conscious of the irrational expectations they have of themselves by practicing mindfulness.

A key element of mindfulness is meditation, which offers people a disciplined approach to cultivating self-acceptance and self-compassion. People who regularly practice meditation may break free from the never-ending pressure to perform flawlessly and instead concentrate on developing their self-awareness and self-care. It encourages people to accept their flaws without passing judgment on them and to develop a self-worth independent of accomplishments outside of oneself.

Perfectionists who practice meditation may learn to let go of their crippling fear of failing and adopt a more balanced, healthy attitude to their aspirations. With time, these techniques may lessen the detrimental effects of perfectionism on mental health, fostering improved well-being and a more contented and laid-back lifestyle.

Being a Perfectionist with Self-Compassion
Being kind and patient with oneself, particularly in the face of failure or perceived deficiencies, is a key component of developing self-compassion. The self-talk and self-criticism that are often connected to perfectionism may be mitigated by engaging in self-compassion practices. One may learn to accept shortcomings and lessen the negative effects of perfectionism on their mental health by developing a more understanding and caring attitude toward oneself.

Being a Perfectionist and Setting Realistic Goals
Perfectionists often establish impossible standards for themselves, which exacerbates emotions of disappointment and failure. Without always aiming for perfection, people may achieve balance and a feeling of success by learning to create objectives that are clear, attainable, and time-bound.

People may lessen the overwhelming strain that sometimes accompanies perfectionism by breaking major activities down into smaller, achievable stages. This method makes possible:

A feeling of success
Reinforcement of a constructive feedback loop that
Boosts confidence and motivation
Enhanced flexibility and durability
Acknowledgment that errors and failures are inevitable in every undertaking

People learn to regard errors as chances for learning and development rather than as fatalities, which progressively lessens the crippling dread of making mistakes that often afflicts perfectionists.

In the end, having realistic objectives promotes a more positive self-perception of one's talents and increases happiness in both the personal and professional spheres.

Seeking Assistance as an Overachiever
For people who struggle with perfectionism, reaching out to friends, family, or mental health experts may be a great source of help. Individuals may benefit from discussing difficulties and exchanging experiences:

➔ *Obtain perspective*
➔ *Create coping mechanisms*
➔ *Feel less alone in their endeavors*

Since perfectionism is a problem that most individuals in the United States report having, there's a good chance that a close friend or relative will be able to relate to you. This kind of intimate support network may help you not only deal with your perfectionism more effectively, but it can also expose you to fresh, insightful, and tried-and-true methods that others have successfully handled.

Being a Perfectionist and Getting a Growth Mindset
Adopting a development mindset entails prioritizing advancement over perfection. People may cultivate a more positive outlook on success and accomplishment by realizing that errors and setbacks are chances for development.

The idea that one's skills and intellect can be enhanced and expanded by work, education, and persistence is known as a growth mindset. Those with a growth mindset handle difficulties and learn more positively and adaptively than those with a fixed mentality, which holds that an individual's qualities and talents are permanent and unchanging.

People who have a growth mentality often see obstacles as chances for personal development rather than as dangers to their self-worth. Rather than seeing mistakes and losses as signs of their innate inadequacies, they view them as important learning opportunities. This viewpoint motivates individuals to persevere through hardship, putting in the work necessary to acquire new abilities and accomplish their objectives. Furthermore, those who have a growth mindset are more likely to ask for and welcome criticism because they perceive it as an opportunity to become better rather than a reflection of their skills.

On a personal level, developing a growth mindset may improve one's general feeling of well-being and empower people to pursue their goals with more zeal and tenacity. In the end, embracing a growth mindset enables people to reach their greatest potential and face obstacles in life with more optimism and resiliency.

Developing Resilience while Pursuing Perfection
Overcoming perfectionism requires building resilience. The capacity to overcome obstacles and adjust to difficult situations is resilience. Through developing resilience, people may learn to see failure as a necessary learning opportunity and a normal part of life rather than as a catastrophic blow to their self-worth.

Getting Expert Assistance for Perfectionism

For a lot of people, getting professional assistance can be required to address the underlying problems that are causing their perfectionism. To overcome perfectionistic inclinations and manage related mental health difficulties, help and support may be obtained from a mental health professional, such as a psychiatrist or psychologist.

Patients may discover the causes of their problem, whether they are social influences, early experiences, or other circumstances, with the assistance of therapists and mental health specialists who specialize in treating perfectionism. People may start to question and reframe their perfectionistic thinking and replace it with more realistic and self-compassionate viewpoints by learning about these roots.

In addition, seeking professional assistance provides a secure and accepting environment in which people may examine the concerns of rejection, failure, or criticism that underpin perfectionism. Counselors may assist patients in:

➜ *Creating Adaptive Response Plans*
➜ *Techniques for managing stress*
➜ *Exercises that boost self-esteem*

→ *Acquiring the capacity for self-compassion*

Therapy may also provide continuous accountability and support as people strive to establish and meet more reasonable standards for themselves. Ultimately, getting professional assistance for perfectionism may be a transformative experience that helps people escape the vicious cycle of procrastination and perfectionism while also promoting improved mental and emotional health.

Exploring the Perils and Strategies of Perfectionism

Perils of Perfectionism:
• Procrastination: Perfectionists may delay tasks due to fear of not meeting high standards, leading to missed opportunities and increased stress.
• Burnout: The pursuit of perfection can lead to exhaustion and burnout, negatively impacting physical and emotional well-being.
• Strained Relationships: Perfectionists' critical nature and unrealistic expectations can strain relationships, leading to conflict and isolation.
• Diminished Creativity: Fear of failure and rigid thinking can stifle creativity and innovation.
• Low Self-Esteem: Constant self-criticism can erode self-esteem and undermine confidence.

Impact on Mental Health:
• Anxiety: Perfectionists often experience heightened levels of anxiety due to the fear of making mistakes or falling short of their standards.
• Depression: Persistent feelings of inadequacy and failure can contribute to depression.

Strategies for Overcoming Perfectionism:

• Cognitive Behavioral Therapy (CBT): CBT helps identify and challenge perfectionistic beliefs and behaviors, promoting adaptive coping strategies.

• Meditation and Mindfulness: Practices like meditation and mindfulness can increase self-awareness and reduce self-critical thoughts.

• Setting Realistic Goals: Establishing achievable goals and focusing on progress can alleviate pressure to be flawless.

• Seeking Support: Building a support network can provide encouragement and guidance.

• Developing a Growth Mindset: Viewing mistakes as opportunities for learning and growth.

• Building Resilience: Developing resilience helps individuals bounce back from setbacks and challenges.

• Professional Assistance: Seeking therapy or counseling can provide personalized support and strategies.

Can a relationship be ruined by perfectionism?

10 ways perfectionism damages relationship

Can you overcome perfectionism in relationships?

Perfectionists project social expectations onto themselves, believing that no matter how well they perform, the audience expects more from them. This tendency is known as a projection of social pressures onto oneself. That fuels the quest for **"perfect perfection."**

In relationships, perfectionism may be both dangerous and rewarding. A person desires a partner who pushes them to be the greatest versions of themselves while also providing encouragement and support.

The issue with dating a perfectionist is that they expect the relationship and both of you to live up to their exaggerated standards of perfection.

That will not only be bad for your mental health but also theirs, and it will probably lead to the breakup of the relationship.

Since communication and compromise are the cornerstones of a real relationship, the perfectionist would have to "overcome" their inclination toward perfection.

Establishing a connection with true needs requires honesty, openness, and devotion toward realistic expectations. It may be difficult to overcome the perfectionist's perspective, but it is essential for a good relationship.

Can a relationship be ruined by perfectionism?
A relationship might be ruined by someone who suffers from perfectionism as the expectations are so high that a partner cannot live up to them.

You will undoubtedly feel like a failure since perfection is what you strive for. You put this onto your spouse, making you despise them, which can only be detrimental to your relationship.

Attempt this as well: Are You a Perfectionist in Your Partnership?

What are some ways that relationships are impacted by perfectionism?

In a relationship, perfectionism demands that a partner live up to the same expectations as the mate does. That implies that failure is all but certain and that the significant other will never be able to live up to their expectations.

See some of the ways that romantic perfectionism may be undermining your relationship:

1. It's hard for your spouse to please you
You are never completely pleased in a relationship because of the irrational expectations you have for your spouse, yourself, and the relationship as a whole. Perfectionism in partnerships is impossible to achieve.

2. There is constant disagreement and resentment
Even if you want your relationship to be perfect—full of love and happiness—there will always be arguments and discord when someone messes up or falls short of your very high expectations.

3. The connection does not include forgiveness.
Expectations are fulfilled when you live with a perfectionist because anything less is undesirable, unbearable, and unforgivable. When someone "fails," the perfectionist believes they stand to lose too much, hence they are not tolerant.

4. There is no intermediate state; anything is either
It seems as if there are no "gray areas" when attempting to identify perfectionism in a relationship—it's either there or it isn't. No matter how many things a spouse does to show they love you if they violate an intention, it is assumed that they don't love you.

5. Your heart is not always in the individual.
When you work toward the "goal" of love with a spouse, you come to value the concept of "love" and achieve that ideal above your actual relationship. That will inevitably cause harm to someone.

How to Prevent Perfectionism's Negative Effects on Relationships

1. You don't feel great about the change
You're not good with spontaneity since you like to be in charge. You want everything to be well-organized and stay that way. Anything that deviates from that should alarm you.

2. Sometimes it's necessary to compare
A partner in a relationship is held to the highest standards due to perfectionism. How are you aware of these? You want to outperform everyone else in your relationship by comparing it to what you think it should be.

Once again, it is irrational since nobody can know what takes on with another couple behind closed doors. You assume and hold your partner responsible even though your connection doesn't seem to be as solid.

3. Unfavorable to your partner
Your partner should aim for perfection to be the finest version of themselves, in line with your perfectionist worldview. You are just as harsh on your spouse as you would be on yourself when they do poorly or pass up a chance.

4. Scorecards are kept in the mind
Similarly, rather than just berating your spouse for perceived shortcomings, you record their errors in a "mental notebook."

5. Discord indicates a lack of success
Conflict arises naturally in most good relationships when passion, viewpoints, and emotions are acknowledged.

That does not imply that you will fight all the time or that you will have to see the therapist.

Any discussion of dispute is seen as a failure in partnerships when perfectionism and anxiety are present. This kind of thinking implies that relationships should always be "sunshine and daisies."

6. A lack of dialogue or compromise
A feeling of normality that would allow for open communication and compromise on problems gets in the way of a successful partnership when perfectionism is present in close relationships.

A perfectionist does not believe in compromising on their ideal; instead, they like to have everything under control and in a tidy little package.

7. The bad is often highlighted rather than the positive
When someone is a perfectionist in a relationship, they often overlook their partner's positive traits and focus primarily on their flaws. Since the majority of happiness and satisfaction comes from the small things, you lose out on such things.

Everybody will sometimes make mistakes. It doesn't make you so flawless when you concentrate on something and make it enormous while ignoring what works. You make a portion of that person disintegrate.

8. Your withdrawal hurts your partner as well.
Because you're afraid you won't say or do the right thing, or because you may not look the part, you prefer to avoid social circles, family, and friends. This makes you remain at home and upset your spouse because you miss out on time with their close friends or family.

When a partner stops participating in social activities, they may get angry, feel bored, or even start to worry about not going out and having fun.

9. The "baseline" is the honeymoon period.
The perfectionist's honeymoon period is what they consider to be the perfect representation of what love should be: addicting, intoxicating, thrilling, and something they want to hang onto, even if it means finding a new partner with whom the bliss could last longer.

Sadly, the flawed attitude of the perfectionist ignores the fact that being committed to your partner and in a relationship over time is not the same as just falling in love. You'll never locate the perfect attachment version unless you can understand those distinctions.

10. The hallmark of a perfectionist is procrastination
When it comes to relationships, perfectionism implies that your partner will have to wait on you a lot since you usually put things off. After all, there's always the dread of not succeeding in whatever you do.

There are times when you decide not to try at all because you are so afraid of failing or making errors. That is self-defeating in and of itself, a kind of failure due to caving into fear.

Is it possible to go over perfectionism in a relationship? An important first step in changing the habit is realizing that you are experiencing perfectionism in your relationships.

Most people are dealing with some kind of emotional distress, trauma, or even a habit that they need to accept to move on in their relationships and lives healthily.

How can we solve the puzzle and go forward? Some people never identify the reason for their ongoing relationship failures. Even so, it's a good idea to act on it, either on your own or in treatment with a counselor, or even just look for the resources you'll need to solve the problem.

Several strategies to help you quit being a perfectionist; after that, you may want to get in touch with an expert who can provide you with further advice.

1. Give up making assumptions about your partner's past way of life.
If you're looking for ways to overcome your perfectionism, giving up on the idea that your partner had a better life than you would be a great place to start. You are competing with an image that you do not know of, and you are projecting this onto your spouse, who has no idea how you are thinking.

Recognizing that this individual is with you is crucial. It makes no difference whether their ex-partner was in superior physical or mental health. The best method to get the information you need is to communicate. The words must be accepted as given and then released.

Overcoming Perfectionism in Relationships

Practice Self-Compassion:
• Treat yourself with kindness and understanding.
• Develop a forgiving and accepting attitude towards yourself and your partner.

Communicate Openly:
• Foster open and honest communication in your relationship.
• Prevent misunderstandings and build trust.

Focus on the Positive:
• Celebrate each other's strengths and accomplishments.
• Express gratitude for the love and support shared.

Set Realistic Expectations:
• Acknowledge that no one is perfect, including yourself and your partner.
• Set realistic expectations for your relationship.

Seek Professional Help:

• Seek guidance and support from a therapist or counselor if perfectionism continues to negatively impact your relationship.

Practice Mindfulness:
• Incorporate mindfulness practices into your daily routine.

Celebrate Progress:
• Celebrate the progress you make in overcoming perfectionism.

Focus on Growth:
• Shift focus from achieving perfection to personal and relational growth.

Be Patient:
• Overcoming perfectionism is a process that takes time and effort.

Can a pair of perfectionists coexist?

**Why Two People Who Are Perfect For Each Other
Fail To Make A Relationship Work**

This is how it impacts your partnership:

1. You have a strict opinion on how things ought to be.
Perfectionists care more about the ideal state of affairs than the actual state of affairs. Instead of observing their partner for who they are, they consider if they would meet their idealized version of them.

2. You have exaggerated expectations.
They place excessive strain on their relationships because they have strong opinions about how their partners should act, appear, and perform. Your relationship suffers as a consequence.

3. You think there shouldn't be any arguments or disputes in the relationship.

You define an ideal relationship as one in which there are no disagreements or disputes. In the actual world of ties and human emotions, it is not that way. Because perfectionism thrives on feelings of inadequacy and insecurity, disagreement may make people feel very uncomfortable.

4. Your propensity to be critical of oneself while elevating others

They struggle to appreciate and be present in the moment because they have a constant inner critic. "Future tasks and things to do usually dominate the internal dialogue in the head, which causes guilt and frustration that is then projected onto other people as well.

5. You're not very forgiving.

Perfectionists have a hard time forgiving others after they have forgiven themselves. They have so high expectations of themselves that everything that doesn't live up to them is considered a failure. They also feel inferior to anything that symbolizes failure, thus they would stop at nothing to escape it.

Therefore, try not to seek perfection from others, from oneself, or relationships. Seek out the pleasures in imperfection, acknowledge one other's little frailties, cherish diversity, and welcome disagreements. That is an indication of a strong partnership. It's perfectly OK to be faulty!

Chapter Summary

Imperfectionism's Impact on Relationships

• Rigid Expectations: Perfectionists may set unrealistic expectations, leading to disappointment and frustration.

• High Standards: They may set high standards, causing constant dissatisfaction.

• Avoidance of Conflict: They may struggle with conflict resolution, viewing disagreements as failures.

• Self-Criticism: They may overly criticize themselves, causing feelings of insecurity and unworthiness.

• Lack of Forgiveness: They may struggle to forgive themselves and others, leading to resentment and bitterness.

• Fostering Healthy Relationships: Embrace imperfection, practice forgiveness, and communicate openly.

Read Me

Kudos!!!

How was the journey through this guide?

I'm pretty sure this guide is helpful in one way or the other. In respect to that, do well to drop a Global Rating Star or a simple message to me through the Review writing provided area.

Furthermore, a title called "Psychology of dbt studies" will also be helpful in one way or the other. So, I suggest you go through it and apply the extracted knowledge in it.

Tucker Cares.